Doodle Dandy!

The Complete Book of Independence Day Words

By Lynda Graham-Barber

Pictures by Betsy Lewin

★ ★ ★

BRADBURY PRESS / NEW YORK

Maxwell Macmillan Canada / Toronto
Maxwell Macmillan International
New York / Oxford / Singapore / Sydney

Bradbury Press
Macmillan Publishing Company
866 Third Avenue
New York, NY 10022

Maxwell Macmillan Canada, Inc.
1200 Eglinton Avenue East
Suite 200
Don Mills, Ontario M3C 3N1

Macmillan Publishing Company is part of the
Maxwell Communication Group of Companies.

First edition
Printed and bound in the United States of America

10 9 8 7 6 5 4 3 2 1

Book design by Cathy Bobak

Library of Congress Cataloging-in-Publication Data
Graham-Barber, Lynda.
Doodle Dandy! : the complete book of Independence Day words / by
Lynda Graham-Barber ; pictures by Betsy Lewin.—1st ed.
p.   cm.
Includes bibliographical references and index.
Summary: Defines or explains various words commonly associated
with Independence Day, such as "barbecue," "fireworks," and
"liberty," and gives their origin or historical background.
ISBN 0-02-736675-8
1. Fourth of July—Juvenile literature.   2. United States—
History—Revolution, 1775–1783—Juvenile literature.   3. English
language—Etymology—Juvenile literature.   [1. Fourth of July.
2. English language—Etymology.]   I. Lewin, Betsy, ill.   II. Title.
E286.A1298   1992
394.2'68473—dc20   91-19409

In loving memory of my father,
Emerson C. Graham, U.S.A.F.,
who was born on the Fourth of July

The first of earthly blessings, independence
—EDWARD GIBBON

CONTENTS

Happy INDEPENDENCE DAY!
JULY fourth is America's
BIRTHDAY.

INDEPENDENCE DAY

Happy birthday, America! It's July fourth, and from coast to coast the country is getting ready to celebrate. Can you smell the suntan lotion and the grilled hot dogs? Red, white, and blue bunting stretches across parade review stands, and nervous baton twirlers get in some last-minute practice. Swimming pools expect a capacity crowd, and local chambers of commerce and businesses are preparing fireworks displays that will serve as the explosive finale to America's annual salute to liberty.

July fourth has traditionally been the day we celebrate Independence Day. The word *independence* is made up of *in-* "not" and *dependence*. Dependence comes from the Latin word *pendère*, "to hang from," or "to dwell upon." Dependence is a state in which people "hang from," or are influenced by, others. The condition of not "hanging onto" someone or something else is called independence.

It was in Philadelphia on July 4, 1776, that the fifty-six delegates to the Second Continental Congress voted to adopt the Declaration of Independence. This document declared that the thirteen colonies had officially broken their ties with England.

But the congressional delegates had already decided two

days earlier, on July 2, that "these United Colonies are, and of right ought to be, free and independent states."

John Adams thought July 2 would go down in history as the date to celebrate the country's national birthday. A letter from John Adams to his wife confirms this: "The Second of July, 1776, will be the most memorable epoch in the history of America. . . . It ought to be solemnized with pomp and parade, with shows . . . bonfires and illuminations, from one end of this continent to the other. . . . I am apt to believe that it will be celebrated by succeeding generations as the great anniversary festival."

So why did the Fourth of July become the date of the "great anniversary festival" with all the pomp and celebration?

Even though the colonies voted to be independent on July 2, it wasn't until July 4, after two days of studying the Declaration of Independence, that the Congress took the official vote and approved the document. But even then, there was little hoopla in Philadelphia. On a stormy July 4, 1776, there were, surprisingly, no parties or fireworks to mark the day. There are no accounts of the Liberty Bell ringing. Why not? Quite simply, there was work to be done, and the country and its leaders took their task seriously.

After Congress had adopted the declaration and John Hancock signed it, printers worked overtime running off copies of the document and riders saddled their horses to deliver the copies to the people. To help spread the word, the Declaration of Independence was published in the Philadelphia *Evening Post* on July 6. But it wasn't until July 8 that the declaration was read publicly in Independence Square. After the reading, John Adams made this observation: "Three cheers rended the Welkin [sky]. The Battalions paraded on the common, and gave Us the Feu de Joy [gun salute] notwithstanding the Scarcity of Powder" (for the muskets).

At last, some noise and commotion. But the battle for freedom was not over. Before the young nation could confirm its independence, a bloody war would be fought, spanning seven years, from the musket that fired the "shot heard round the world" at Lexington, to the last drum roll at Yorktown.

During these turbulent years, patriots and redcoats met in

fierce battles, the stars and stripes banner was created, and celebrated Americans like George Washington, Paul Revere, Betsy Ross, and Thomas Jefferson helped forge a new future for America.

To find the root for July, the seventh month of the year, we must go back to ancient Rome, to one of its most famous emperors, Julius Caesar, who lived from July 12, 100 B.C., to March 15, 44 B.C. The Latin name *Julius* became in Old English *Julius*, in Middle English *Julie*, and finally in modern English *July*. Up until the nineteenth century, July was pronounced to rhyme with "truly," or with the name Julie.

In 46 B.C., two years before he was assassinated, Julius Caesar set up a new calendar. This calendar, which the ruler called the Julian, after himself, established a year made up of twelve months and three hundred and sixty-five days.

Not only did Caesar have a namesake calendar, but it's believed that his general Mark Antony (ca. 83–30 B.C.) may have changed the name of the month in which Caesar was born, Quintilis, to July, as a way of honoring the slain ruler after he died. English scholar Philemon Holland (1552–1637) writes about it this way in *Suetonius, Lives of the Caesars*: "Caesar . . . was born . . . upon the fourth day before the Ides of Quintilis, which month, after his death, was by virtue of the law Antonia (Antony) called for that cause, July."

 Do You Know

The Julian calendar in use at the time of the Roman republic consisted of twelve lunar months: Martius, Aprilis, Maius, Iunius, Quintilis, Sextilis, September, October, November, December, Januarius, Februarius. At this time Quintilis, which became July, was the fifth month of the year. To these ancient Romans, the year began on March 1, or Martius 1. It wasn't until 153 B.C. that January and February were moved to the beginning of the year and January 1 officially became New Year's Day.

Although we look forward to picnics and swimming in July, the July of 1816 in the Northeast was an exception. During this July people wore heavy overcoats. In fact, there had been a killing frost each month that year. Faced with starvation, many people in the Northeast left their homes. Although there is no official explanation for this freakish weather, one probable cause may have been the eruption of a volcano in Indonesia. It's believed that the ash from the eruption blocked out the sun's rays. Europe also experienced an unusually cold summer in 1816. With food in short supply, many people subsisted on a diet of fish, and 1816 became known as the mackerel year.

Scientists predict that after Mount Pinatubo's eruption in the Philippines in June 1991, a similar haze will affect global temperatures. The haze, which reflects and scatters sunlight, could lower average temperatures by more than half a degree Fahrenheit for a period of three to four years.

BIRTHDAY

The origins of the word *birthday* go back to the word *byrth*, which meant "the bearing of offspring" in Old Norse, the North Germanic language of the Scandinavian peoples, and the Old English word *daeg*, "day," or the "time of sunlight."

When we celebrate the annual observance of someone's day of birth, we call it their birthday. To commemorate birthdays we offer birthday greetings with cards, gifts, and cakes. Often we put on our good clothes for a birthday party. Do we wear, then, a birthday suit, as English doctor-turned-writer Tobias Smollett (1721–1771) wrote about in his rowdy novel *The Adventures of Ferdinand Count Fathom*? "He made an apology for receiving the count in his birthday suit." Today, the term "birthday suit" is a humorous way of referring to bare skin. But in Smollett's time it meant literally the special suit of clothing worn on the king of England's birthday.

As we have read, the actual birthday of America—July 4, 1776—was not a day marked with fireworks and celebrations. The first grand birthday celebration occurred in Philadelphia July 4, 1777. Then bells rang everywhere, bonfires blazed, and fireworks illuminated the skies. Ships fired off thirteen-gun salutes, and every house in the city displayed a burning candle in the front window. Even Congress adjourned its regular business on that special day.

✦ ✦ FAMOUS *FOURTH OF JULY* EVENTS ✦ ✦

WHEN	WHERE	WHAT HAPPENED
July 4, 1778	Paris	First overseas celebration of America's independence, with John Adams and Benjamin Franklin attending
July 4, 1834	New York City	Riots at antislavery protests
July 4, 1876	Philadelphia	First American international exposition; 236 acres of exhibits; 10 million attend
July 4, 1883	North Platte, Nebraska	First Wild West Show, starring Buffalo Bill Cody
July 4, 1903	Pecos, Texas	First rodeo with prizes; President Theodore Roosevelt opens first Pacific cable
July 4, 1946	Washington, D.C.	President Truman declares the independence of the Philippines
July 4, 1959	Washington, D.C.	First 49-star flag raised, with Alaska the new state

BOYCOTT

If you refuse to buy ivory because the primary source of commercial ivory, the African elephant, is an endangered species, then you are boycotting ivory. Whenever you boycott something, you hope to put pressure on the person or group responsible for the product, service, or belief.

The word *boycott* came directly from the name of the man who, by some twist of irony, was himself the victim of a boycott in Ireland in 1880. His name was Captain Charles Cunningham Boycott (1832–1897). Captain Boycott collected rents from his tenants, and he imposed strict payment schedules. In the fall of 1880, the tenants protested by refusing to work for their landlord, Captain Boycott. As a result, his servants fled, his fences were destroyed, and his food supplies were cut off.

The term *boycott* was quickly picked up by the English newspapers as a way of describing threatening actions like the ones against Captain Boycott. An 1880 issue of the *Illustrated London News* carried this entry: "To Boycott has already become a verb active, signifying to intimidate . . . and to taboo."

The American colonists staged several boycotts against England during the 1760s and 1770s. The boycotts were a means of protesting what they felt were unfair taxes imposed on them by England. In addition to being forbidden to manufacture and sell goods that would compete with English products, the colonies were taxed on many goods imported into the colonies. Why should they, the colonists argued, pay English taxes when they had no representation in the government of Great Britain?

But after long and expensive wars with France, including the French and Indian War in North America, England was faced with an empty treasury. High taxes in England were not enough; officials repeatedly taxed the American colonies in an attempt to reduce England's enormous war debt.

Here are a few of the taxes placed on the colonies and how Americans reacted to them.

DATE	TAX/ACT	MEASURES
1763	Molasses Act	Tax added to every gallon of molasses imported into the colonies

Result: The price of rum, made from molasses, increases. Colonists begin an illegal trade in foreign molasses. The act is revised three years later.

DATE	TAX/ACT	MEASURES
1764	Sugar Act	Puts duty on foreign refined sugar; colonists are prohibited from importing French wine or foreign rum

Result: British planters now have monopoly in American sugar market. Colonists boycott luxury goods from England, including lace and ruffles. The act is revised, together with the Molasses Act.

DATE	TAX/ACT	MEASURES
1765	Stamp Act	All legal papers (newspapers, marriage licenses, diplomas, ships' papers, etc.) are taxed and must carry a large blue seal or "stamp" as proof of payment

Result: Riots erupt in New York City and Boston. Stamp masters are threatened while selling stamps. No ship papers are stamped, so transatlantic trade halts. The act is repealed.

DATE	TAX/ACT	MEASURES
1767	Townshend Acts	Taxes set on English imports of lead, glass, paints, paper, and tea

Result: Colonists boycott all English manufactured items—a great sacrifice, since they have not been allowed to produce their own goods. Colonists begin weaving their own clothing. Coffee drinking increases. The act is repealed.

DATE	TAX/ACT	MEASURES
1773	Tea Act	Duty on tea retained

Result: Colonists impose an embargo on all tea taxed from England. Angry patriots chop open tea chests from three English ships and dump the tea leaves into Boston Harbor.

COLONY

The word *colony* developed from the Latin word *colon*, meaning "farmer or settler in a new country." In Latin a *colonia* was a farm, and in both Middle English and Old French the word evolved into *colonie*.

In the midsixteenth century, when you referred to "the colonies," you meant a farm or rural settlement, as in this line from English writer William Painter's (1540?–1594) collection of tales *The Palace of Pleasure*: "The rural people abandoning their colonies fled for rescue into the city."

In modern usage, a colony became a settlement in a new country, like the colonies settled by the English who immigrated to America. As a group, these thirteen colonies formed the United Colonies. The thirteen American colonies were as diverse as the people who inhabited them. During the American war for independence, the British generals were frustrated by this diversity and, as a result, were never sure where to focus their attacks.

But these dissimilarities also proved a liability, in that each colony had different goals. John Adams (1735–1826), delegate to both the first and second Continental Congresses and who later became president, said, "Winning the American Revolution is like trying to make thirteen clocks strike at once."

The thirteen colonies in order of founding are:

Virginia   1607
Massachusetts   1629
New Hampshire   1629
Maryland   1632
Connecticut   1662
Rhode Island   1663
North Carolina   1663
South Carolina   1663
New York   1664
New Jersey   1665
Pennsylvania   1681
Delaware   1703 (separates from Pennsylvania)
Georgia   1732

 Do You Know

Colony, *protectorate*, *dominion*, and *territory* are words that each represent a group or area with a slightly different status. A colony is made up of a group of people who leave one country to settle another, such as the English people who settled the thirteen colonies in America. If a state or power is looked after by a larger, stronger power (presumably to prevent it from being overtaken) the protected area is called a protectorate. A dominion is specifically a British colony still tied to England but self-governing, like Canada and Australia. Territory is a status given to certain areas of a country that are usually remote and relatively undeveloped, as, for example, the Yukon Territory in Canada's far north.

The word *state* descended from the Roman word *status*, which means "condition" and "manner of standing." When someone has "standing" in the community, he or she is said to have status.

This country is made up of fifty states (and the District of Columbia), all united under one federal government. A state is a unit, or part, of a larger nation. In order to have a state, there must be people, a defined territory, and a government that enacts a state constitution and laws for the individual states. For example, if you live in California, you are subject to the laws of the state of California, in addition to those of the federal government.

UNITE

The basis for the word *unite* is the Latin word *unire*, "to join together," from the Latin root *unus*, meaning "one," which evolved in Old French as *unite*. Sometimes people unite, or clasp, their hands together when they make their marriage vows. Countries also unite either in war, or peace, as in this example from English dramatist and poet William Shakespeare's (1564–1616) *2 Henry IV* (act IV, scene 1, lines 222–3): "Our peace will, like a broken limb united, Grow stronger for the breaking."

19

The United States of America

Meeting in Philadelphia on September 9, 1776, the Continental Congress passed a resolution that changed the name of the nation from the United Colonies to the United States.

It was patriot pamphleteer Thomas Paine (1737–1809) who expanded the name to the United States of America, and he was the first person to use the name in print. Although now considered a champion of patriotism and individual rights, Paine was later in his life denounced in the colonies as a radical atheist and slanderer. Disgraced, he died in poverty. This prophetic warning of Paine's is typical of the inflammatory remarks that got him into trouble: "The United States of America will sound as pompously in the world or in history as The Kingdom of Great Britain."

The new nation called itself the United States of America, but does that mean the states were united in their opposition to England? Over half a million colonists sided with King George III (1738–1820), and right up until the final decision on the Declaration of Independence, there was squabbling among the delegates as to how they would vote.

American poet Walt Whitman (1819–1892) put it this way in his book of poetry *Leaves of Grass*: "The United States themselves are essentially the greatest poem. . . . Here at last is something in the doings of man that corresponds with the broadcast doings of the day and night."

 Do You Know

In 1604, King James I issued a gold coin in England. It had an original value of twenty shillings and was called a unite in reference to the union of the Scottish and English crowns under James, who was Scottish.

REPRESENTATION

The word *representation* presented itself in English from the Latin word *praesentare*, "to bring, or introduce, before someone." *Praesentare* evolved in Middle English as *representen* and *representation* in French.

When you elect officers to the student council, their job is to represent you in bringing, or introducing, your views before the administration. Elected officers represent the different views of the entire student body. Today voters in the United States elect local and state representatives who offer voters' opinions in the House of Representatives and the Senate.

The United States Constitution of 1787 created a Congress with two houses—the Senate and House of Representatives—and a judicial system with the Supreme Court at its head. In the first Congress of 1789, there were sixty-five members in the House of Representatives. The number of representatives in the House is based on the ratio of an area's population to that of the entire country. In 1910 the ratio was set at one state representative for every 200,000 people. A 1929 act set the total number of House seats at 435. Each state, irrespective of population, sends two senators to the Senate.

Artistic works are also called representations because they offer, or depict, an image or thought. Representative Stan Fore decided against buying the painting, which depicted a handsome representation of Uncle Sam, because it represented too big an investment for him.

 Do You Know

All states except Nebraska have law-making bodies that are divided into two houses, or chambers—a legislature and a general assembly. Nebraska has only one chamber, and all officials are referred to as senators. In most states, the upper house is called the Senate and the lower the House of Representatives. State senators are usually elected every four years, while representatives or assembly members are voted on every two years.

BOOM, BANG! Bombs BURST! Sound the ALARM as PATRIOTS and REDCOATS go to BATTLE in the REVOLUTIONARY WAR.

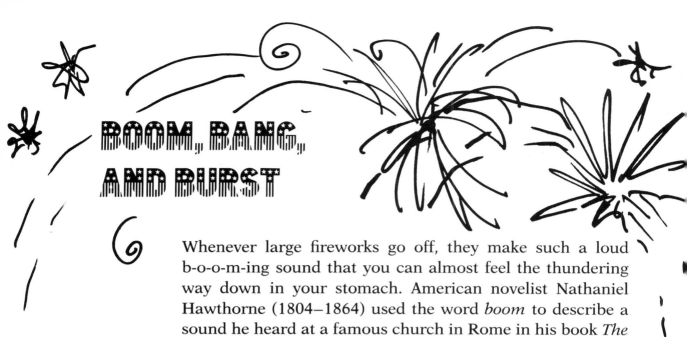

BOOM, BANG, AND BURST

Whenever large fireworks go off, they make such a loud b-o-o-m-ing sound that you can almost feel the thundering way down in your stomach. American novelist Nathaniel Hawthorne (1804–1864) used the word *boom* to describe a sound he heard at a famous church in Rome in his book *The French and Italian Journals of Nathaniel Hawthorne*: "The great bell of St. Peter's tolled with a deep boom."

The word *boom* came into our language because it imitates, or sounds like, the noise that it describes. Such words are said to be onomatopoeic, from the Greek words *onoma*, "name," and *poiein*, "to make." The sound of onomatopoeic words, in effect, create their own names. Other examples of these descriptive words are *whine*, *pop*, *gurgle*, *zip*, and *moan*. Favorite comic book examples include: *zap*! *pow*! *yikes*! and *ouch*!

Booming and banging sounds often occur together. Yet, unlike *boom*, we can clearly trace the history of the word *bang*. It arrived in English from the Old Norse word *banga*, "to hammer," and a Low German word *bangen*, "to strike." The act of firing a gun is also described as a bang, as we read in Richard Henry Dana, Jr.'s (1815–1882) classic sea adventure, *Two Years Before the Mast*: "The watch on deck were banging away at the guns every few minutes."

If you eat too many grilled hot dogs at the Fourth of July barbecue, you might say you feel ready to burst. *Burst* grew out of the Old High German word *brestan*, "to break open." Blisters burst; so do balloons. More poetically, poets write of birds bursting on the wing, hearts bursting, and tears bursting forth when a person is disappointed in love. Franco almost burst into laughter when his leading lady burst into tears after bursting onto the opera set ahead of her cue.

Seven centuries ago, when an alarm sounded—either a cry, a drum, or a bell—the message was clear: get ready to fight. From the Old French word *alarme*, "alarm," and the Italian *allarme*, or *all'arme!*, literally "to the arms!" comes the word *alarm*. Soon *alarm* meant any call or summons. Today we have alarm clocks and smoke alarms, and we become alarmed when a sudden fear overcomes us. Alarmed at his stomach's reaction to a four-alarm chili dinner, Paul set his alarm clock in time to sound the alarm for the patriots.

When we think of *alarm* and the American war for independence, the name Paul Revere (1735–1818) comes to mind. American poet Henry Wadsworth Longfellow's (1807–1882) poem "Paul Revere's Ride" vividly describes the thundering hooves and the famous mud-spattered patriot rider who rode from village to village, alarming the colonists that the British were marching.

The poem is rich in descriptive, dramatic imagery. Here's a sampling:

> A hurry of hoofs in a village street,
> A shape in the moonlight, a bulk in the dark,
> And beneath, from the pebbles, in passing, a spark
> Struck out by a steed flying fearless and fleet;
> That was all! And yet, through the gloom and the light
> The fate of a nation was riding that night;
> And the spark struck out by that steed in his flight
> Kindled the land into flames with its heat.

Although one of early America's most proficient silversmiths, engravers, and political cartoonists, Paul Revere's name will be most remembered for his midnight ride. An experienced horseman, Paul Revere actually made several rides during the early days of the war; the two most significant occurred in April of 1775.

On April 16, having received word that British regulars were being sent to Concord to destroy the colonial munitions,

Paul Revere galloped to Concord to alert the patriots. In case he didn't get through, Revere had arranged to have lanterns hung in the church steeple to warn the people: "One if by land, and two if by sea." One lantern meant that the British had invaded by land, two lanterns meant they had come by sea. Revere, however, made it to Concord.

Late on April 18, Revere set out again, first in a boat across the Charles River. The oars were wrapped in strips from a woman's petticoat to muffle their sound. Once on land, Revere set off at a gallop on a fast horse across the moonlit landscape, rousing the villagers as he rode. Paul Revere arrived in Lexington in time to warn John Hancock (1737–1793) and Samuel Adams (1722–1803) of the British approach. Both leaders went into hiding. Revere then planned to ride on to Concord, but this time he didn't make it. And for all his hard riding, he received five shillings as wages from the colonists.

What happened to him? Revere, along with two other patriot riders, were stopped by the British just outside Lexington en route to Concord. His two companions escaped, but Revere was captured. Before releasing him, the British seized his horse, and Revere walked a mile back to Lexington, where he rescued some documents John Hancock had forgotten.

 Do You Know

Historians agree that Longfellow took a few liberties in his poem. Paul Revere's main objective during his April 18–19 ride was not to rouse the countryside, as Longfellow tells it, but to warn Samuel Adams and John Hancock in Lexington. The poet also transferred events from the ride Revere made two days earlier. The lanterns Longfellow describes in the poem were the ones hung for the April 16 ride. Further, the poet has Paul Revere reach Concord on April 19, but we know that he never made it.

PATRIOTS AND REDCOATS

From the Greek *patrios*, meaning "of one's father," and the Late Latin word *patriota*, "fellow countryman," comes our word *patriot*. As we use the word now, anyone who expresses an abiding love for his country is a patriot.

It was quite the opposite, however, in the first half of the eighteenth century. English historian Horace Walpole (1717–1797) noted in an essay that by 1744: "The name of patriot had become a by-word of derision . . . the most popular declaration which a candidate could make . . . was that he had never been and never would be a patriot."

When General George Washington (1732–1799) took command of the Continental Army on July 3, 1775, he was faced with the challenge of leading thousands of patriots with no military training, whose only uniforms were buckskinned breeches and homespun shirts. The militia's only requirements were that a man be sixteen and provide his own musket. Those militiamen ready to go into battle at a moment's notice were appropriately called minutemen.

By the middle of 1776, many soldiers in the Continental Army had a uniform that consisted of a tricornered hat, wool hunting shirt, leggings, and woolen stockings. Compared to the American forces, especially the militia, the British soldiers were all spit and polish, sporting brilliant red and white uniforms, set with gleaming brass buttons and buckles. These fashionable British soldiers were called redcoats by the Americans. The word *redcoat* is made up of *red*, from the Old English *read*, "red," plus *coat*, Middle English *cote* from Old High German *kozza*, meaning "coarse mantle."

Throughout history red has been associated with blood and fighting. During the American Revolution, the colonial militiamen specialized in surprise attacks on the redcoats as the British marched in strict formation. To the colonials, the red uniforms made easy targets. But brightly colored uniforms had their practical side in battles fought in a traditional, by-the-book manner, with soldiers lined up in mass formations on open battlefields.

The primary weapons in these early wars were muskets. Once fired, muskets produced thick clouds of smoke that obscured the soldiers. Outfitted in brightly colored uniforms, however, commanders and soldiers could more easily identify their own troops amid all the haze and smoke.

 Do You Know

You may have also read about people called Whigs and Tories during the American Revolution. The word *whig* is an abbreviation of *whiggamore*, from the Scottish word *whig*, "to drive," and *mere*, "mare," a female horse. Originally, in midseventeenth century Scotland, cattle rustlers, no doubt on horseback, were called whigs. In 1679 the label was attached to anyone who opposed King James II in favor of a more powerful Parliament. Later, the Whig party became a major political party in England. Toward the end of the nineteenth century, the Whig party became the Liberal party.

Whigs living in the colonies during the American Revolution favored separation from the British Crown.

The word *tory* originally meant "hunter," from the Irish word *toraighe*, "pursuer," from the verb *toir*, "to pursue." In the seventeenth century, dispossessed Irish plunderers who lived by "pursuing" the riches of the English in Ireland were called Tories. In the next century, English people who aligned themselves on the side of royal authority, opposing the parliamentary-reform-minded Whigs, acquired the name Tories. Tory joined Whig as a major political party in England, changing its name to the Conservative party in the early nineteenth century. Today, an English tory—with a small *t*—is considered a conservative, usually with right-wing preferences.

In the American colonies, colonial Tories remained loyal subjects of King George III and did not support the revolution.

The leaders of today's military do not face the disarray confronted by General Washington in organizing local militias and the Continental Army. Over the years, the military in this country has grown into a multitiered unit. Here's a chart to help sort it all out:

army—a major fighting unit trained basically for land combat

regular—a soldier who is paid to serve in the permanent army of a country or state

militia—branch of a more permanent army usually called on in emergencies

infantry—armed soldiers who fight on foot

cavalry—armed soldiers who must move quickly, formerly on horseback, now in motorized vehicles

troop—a group of soldiers, often in a cavalry unit

squad—a small group of soldiers

platoon—two or more squads

company—two or more platoons with a headquarters unit

battery—an artillery (large mobile firearms—i.e., howitzers) unit equal in size to a company

battalion—unit consisting of a headquarters unit and at least two companies or batteries

division—a major self-contained military unit

corps—a unit with two or more divisions and auxiliary services

BATTLE

From Latin *battuere*, "to beat," and Late Latin *battualia*, "military exercise," the word *battle* evolved into Old English as *bataille*, "to fight." Our modern word *battalion*, "a large military unit," is derived from *battle*.

Two of the most-quoted lines in William Shakespeare's works are from *Macbeth* (act I, scene 1, lines 3–4), when the witches stir their cauldron and recite: "When the hurly-burly's done, When the battle's lost and won." Just prior to Shakespeare's time, *hurly-burly*, "a time of strife and tumult," was written *hurlynge* and *burlynge*. *Hurling* has long meant "strife or commotion," and word experts believe that *burly*, meaning "of muscular build," was added merely to reinforce the sound.

Poets often use *battle* in a symbolic way, as in this line from *Defence of Poetry*, an eloquent defense of the creative imagination by English poet Percy Bysshe Shelley (1792–1822): "Poets are . . . the trumpets which sing to battle. . . ."

Today, we use *battle* whenever we speak of any fight or struggle, not only those on the battlefield. We battle everything from solid waste and traffic on the freeway to expanding waistlines.

The first battles of the Revolutionary War occurred on April

19, 1775, at Lexington and Concord, in Massachusetts. Some 2,000 British infantrymen had set out to destroy patriot guns and supplies in Concord. The redcoats marched first into Lexington, where the outnumbered minutemen blocked their path. When the British commander demanded that they surrender their guns, a shot rang out and both sides opened fire. Although neither side was willing to take credit for what became known as the "shot heard round the world," it's believed that a British soldier opened fire when he misheard an order. After the hurly-burly had ended, the patriots had lost eight men.

A few hours later, in nearby Concord, British redcoats exchanged fire with several hundred colonists across the narrow North Bridge. The British retreated, and as they marched back to Boston in strict formation, they were repeatedly ambushed by newly arriving volunteer units. The proud British regulars suffered a humiliating defeat, with nearly 300 dead, wounded, or missing, almost three times the number of patriot casualties.

#

Bunker Hill, Boston, June 17, 1775

With the redcoats in Boston after Lexington and Concord, the Americans tried to place cannons on two strategic hills overlooking Boston, Bunker's and Breed's hills, to drive the British out. But the ammunition-scarce militiamen were defeated by fire from British warships and British infantrymen with bayonets. The battle is considered a Pyrrhic victory for the British, who lost nearly half of their 2,200 men. Pyrrhus was a king of Epirus who suffered such heavy losses in beating the Romans that any battle won at great expense is called a Pyrrhic victory.

Trenton, New Jersey, December 26, 1776

The American forces scored a major victory at Trenton, immortalized in the famous painting "Washington Crossing the Delaware." General Washington led 2,400 frozen colonial troops, their feet wrapped in blood-stained rags, across the Delaware River in small boats during the night. The patriots routed the British troops, some 1,200 Hessians, from their beds in one of the most daring attacks in military history.

Saratoga, New York, October 1777

This battle, regarded as the turning point of the war, pitted British general "Gentleman" Johnny Burgoyne, intent on capturing Albany, against the brilliant general Benedict Arnold (1741–1801). Arnold's men repeatedly drove the British from the battlefield, but they returned with bayonet charges. When British reinforcements arrived, the Americans retreated. Two weeks later, Burgoyne struck again, and in the midst of battle, Arnold galloped onto the field, leading charges despite being wounded in the leg. Burgoyne surrendered a week later.

Yorktown, Virginia, September 28–October 19, 1781

At the last minute, General Washington rushed his troops to Yorktown, where Lord Cornwallis (1738–1805) was fortifying the town. Cornwallis's men, disheartened and confused, abandoned their defenses with little fight and the Americans, allied with the French under the marquis de Lafayette (1757–1834), mounted a heavy assault that forced Cornwallis to retreat. Washington accepted the British general's surrender on October 19, even as fresh redcoat reinforcements approached Yorktown.

 Do You Know

Because England had little luck in recruiting English soldiers to fight in America, they bought soldiers from other countries. Catherine the Great (1729–1796) of Russia turned them down, so England tried Germany. Of the 30,000 German mercenaries paid to fight, more than half were provided by a German nobleman in southwest Germany named the landgrave of Hesse-Cassel. The men from Hesse-Cassel were nicknamed Hessians, a term that eventually applied to all German mercenaries.

Benedict Arnold was daring and egotistical but a true military genius. Why, then, did this brilliant military leader betray his country and try to sell the plans of the fortifications at West Point to the British?

Historians believe it was probably a combination of two motives: Arnold's extravagant habits and a grudge he held against the Continental Army for promoting officers over him and against General Washington, who'd reprimanded him for violating regulations. The British offered General Arnold 20,000 English pounds for the plans.

REVOLUTIONARY

The word *revolutionary* grew from Latin *re*, "back or against," plus *volvere*, "to revolve, or turn," and *ary*, "related to." From its Latin root sprung the Middle English *revolucioun* and the modern French *revolutionnaire*.

Revolutionary thoughts or actions are those that "turn against" the current tide. These actions can bring about sudden and dramatic changes that sometimes lead to a violent confrontation, or *revolution*.

In Jared Sparks's *Life of Gouverneur Morris*, a collection of the writings of the American statesman (1752–1816), Morris stated: "I think government should be founded on stationary and not revolutionary principles." The principles that thirty-three-year-old lawyer Thomas Jefferson (1743–1826) set down in the Declaration of Independence paved the road to revolution.

There are several common misunderstandings about the Revolutionary War. One of them was that the colonists unanimously supported the revolutionary cause. Of the 2 million colonials, some 500,000 were Tory sympathizers. In some battles, more Americans fought for the king than against him. Neither was the war totally a revolution spurred by the poor patriot farmers. Some patriots, among them John Hancock and George Washington, had become very rich landowners from shipping and tobacco.

Another mistaken impression is that the Continental Army confused the British with their Indian-style fighting. Although the local militias resorted to some unorthodox fighting methods, Prussian Baron von Steuben (1730–1794) was hired by General Washington to train the Continental Army in traditional European combat procedures. Besides, the British were no strangers to Indian-style battles, having fought the native Americans for over seventy years in the French and Indian War. Further, it's often mistakenly reported that the colonists, many of whom used rifles, had the advantage of that weapon's superior range and accuracy over the musket. Reloading the rifle, however, was a long and complicated process. Both sides used primarily muskets, but the European muskets had poor aim and were heavier than the American weapon.

 Do You Know

Have you ever heard of the Green Revolution? In the 1960s and 1970s, improved varieties of cereal crops, like wheat and rice, were introduced in developing countries in Asia and Latin America. This wide-scale planting of higher-yield food crops became known as the Green Revolution.

OTHER EIGHTEENTH-CENTURY REVOLUTIONS

The years surrounding the American Revolution saw changes in many parts of the world. Here are a few other places where people demanded rights and independence, amid a backdrop of revolt.

WHEN	WHERE	WHAT HAPPENED
1714	Tripoli, Libya	Libya revolts against Turkish rule and gains its independence
1715	Scotland	Jacobites (supporters of Catholic Stuart kings) revolt against Protestant King George I, a Hanoverian; the uprising is put down by force
1721	Formosa (now Taiwan)	China suppresses revolution on Formosa
1729	Corsica (Mediter-ranean)	The Corsicans, irritated by a new tax, rise in revolt against the government of Italy's Genoa; independence follows

WHEN	WHERE	WHAT HAPPENED
1746	Scotland	Bonnie Prince Charlie (Stuart heir Charles Edward Stuart) loses his bid for the English throne at Culloden Moor and flees to France
1788	Peru	Peruvians rebel against Spanish rule; independence is gained in 1821
1789– 1799	France	Paris mob storms Bastille; thousands guillotined; Louis XVI and queen executed; Napoleon I crowned himself emperor in 1804
1791	Santo Domingo (now Haiti)	Black slaves revolt against French; independence declared in 1804
1790	Belgium	Austrians suppress revolution in Brussels

The Latin word *bellum* means "war." Our adjectives *bellicose* and *belligerent*, which refer to people who are aggressive fighters and troublemakers, developed from this root. The Latin word for "beautiful" is *bellus*. Because of the close, and potentially confusing, similarity between *bellum* and *bellus*, early Latin-speaking people stopped using *bellum* when they spoke of war. Around A.D. 1050, they began to use the Old English word *wyrre*, meaning "war," which is, in turn, from the Old High German word *werran*, "to bring into confusion."

The phrase "the dogs of war" has often been used in books and movies. It appeared first in William Shakespeare's play *Julius Caesar* (act III, scene 1, line 274), when a loyal Mark Antony eloquently demands that war be unleashed to avenge Caesar's murder: "Cry 'Havoc!' and let slip the dogs of war." In Shakespeare's time *havoc* was a military command that meant to massacre without mercy, and a *slip* was a dog's leash.

As we saw earlier, the revolutionary dogs of war were first unleashed at the battles of Lexington and Concord. The following years of conflict saw much bitterness and bloodshed. Without George Washington's wise leadership and courage, the patriots would have surely been defeated. Many military historians also agree that the colonies would not have won without France's help, especially that of French statesman and general the marquis de Lafayette. Reflecting on the war, General Lafayette wrote these moving words: "I am content! America is assured of her independence. Mankind has won its cause; liberty is no longer homeless on earth."

In General Washington's speech to Congress on January 8, 1790, he stated that "To be prepared for war is one of the most effectual means of preserving peace." Getting prepared for the Revolutionary War was one of Washington's most difficult tasks. The odds against him were tremendous.

Great Britain sent some 55,000 professional soldiers, well outfitted and trained, 30,000 of them Hessian mercenaries. Added to this number were the Indians enlisted by the British to fight the patriots and the half-million American Tories still loyal to the king.

A total of over 200,000 American colonials enlisted during the course of the Revolutionary War. The majority of these, however, were militiamen who fought locally for only a short term in defense of their homes and villages. Never did General Washington have a massive buildup of soldiers; in fact, there were never more than 8,000 colonial soldiers in any one battle.

Even General Washington was surprised at the outcome. "It will not be believed," he stated, "that such a force as Great Britain has employed for eight years in this country could be baffled in their plan of subjugating it by numbers infinitely less—composed of men sometimes half-starved, always in rags, without pay, and experiencing at times every species of distress which human nature is capable of undergoing."

Why, then, did the British lose the war?

The single biggest mistake the British made was to abandon the fight in New England for areas in which they anticipated to find more people loyal to the crown, like New York and the South. The South turned out to be just as rebellious as New England. And once in the South, the British further diluted their strength by dividing their troops.

The British were thousands of miles from home, and their lines of communication were long and often confused. The British also underestimated the fighting loyalties of the patriots and overestimated the extent to which Tory sympathizers would help. The vastness of America bewildered the British, who were often caught off guard when new pockets of rebel resistance sprung up. Even though the British captured the four largest cities in the colonies, New York, Philadelphia, Boston, and Charleston, they were not able to control the four cities at once, nor could they control the vast stretches of land in between.

Do You Know

The "losses" in Washington's army were often due to desertion. Over 5,000 militiamen deserted before a battle at Newport, Rhode Island, forcing General Washington to give up his plan to attack. The militia were at a disadvantage far from home. When crops had to be harvested or a baby was due, militiamen often abandoned the fight and returned home. Or they deserted because they did not agree with the battle strategy.

General Washington knew that the country would need skilled soldiers in the event of another war. To meet this demand, West Point Military Academy was established on the former site of General Washington's Revolutionary War headquarters, at a strategic bend in New York's Hudson River. The academy officially opened its doors on Independence Day in 1802 with a class of ten cadets. In 1976 the academy admitted its first female cadets.

Here is a moving postscript to all wars, written by Walt Whitman in his poem "Reconciliation":

> Beautiful that war and all its deeds of carnage must in
> time be utterly lost,
> That the hands of the sisters Death and Night
> incessantly softly wash again, and ever again, this
> soil'd world;
> For my enemy is dead, a man as divine as myself is
> dead. . . .

47

The FOUNDING FATHERS sign
the DECLARATION OF
INDEPENDENCE,
proclaiming LIBERTY.
FREEDOM, JUSTICE, and
EQUALITY
are America's goals.

FOUNDING FATHERS

At the time of the American Revolution, those men who established the new government were referred to as founding fathers. *Founding* has its root in the Latin word *fundus*, "bottom, or base" and Middle English *founden*; *father* is from the Latin *pater* and, later, Old English *foeder* and Middle English *fader*. These American founding fathers worked to create basic laws and documents from the foundation, or the bottom, up.

As we know, the founding father largely responsible for writing the Declaration of Independence was Thomas Jefferson, who later became president. Jefferson strongly believed that power in the new government should rest with the states and in the people's right to govern themselves through the election of representative leaders. He was the first leader, or father, of the Democratic-Republican party. One of his main political opponents was another founding father, John Adams.

John Adams was a member of the Federalist party, a group that, unlike Jefferson's party, favored a strong, centralized national government. Amazingly enough, both John Adams and Thomas Jefferson, old political enemies who made peace later in their lives, died on July 4, 1826, on the very day America was celebrating the fiftieth anniversary of the Declaration of Independence.

History has accorded another founding father, Benjamin Franklin (1706–1790), a special title—the wisest American. The son of a candle maker, he came to Philadelphia with one dollar in his pocket, and by the age of twenty-three he owned a newspaper—the *Pennsylvania Gazette*. His many diverse accomplishments include inventor (bifocals, an improved stove, water harmonica, lightning rod), diplomat to France, and postmaster of Philadelphia.

A wealthy shipowner, John Hancock was one of most vocal critics of King George III's taxes. For his belligerence, the king put this founding father at the top of his list of most dangerous Americans. A delegate to the Second Continental Congress from Massachusetts, John Hancock was later elected its president. One of John Hancock's most famous duties was to sign the Declaration of Independence. In order to annoy the king, he signed his name in huge letters with many flourishes. Because John Hancock wrote his signature so prominently, the term "John Hancock" has come to refer to a person's signature.

The day Ben founded the first Annual Holly Triathlon, he put his John Hancock on a marriage license and then, with his new bride and her father, watched Father Christmas lead the holiday parade.

Do You Know

Jefferson's Democratic-Republican party became the Democratic party under Andrew Jackson (1767–1845). The Federalists, as established by John Adams, changed their name to the National Republicans in 1828, under the leadership of John Adams's son John Quincy Adams (1767–1848), before becoming simply the Republican party in 1856, under Abraham Lincoln (1809–1865).

DECLARATION OF INDEPENDENCE

The word *declaration* came into our language from the French *declaration*, which evolved from the Latin *declarare*, "to make clear." There are many different kinds of both verbal and written declarations, some less formal than others. "I declare!" said Delia as she completed her customs declaration form, "if I pay all this duty I'll have to declare bankruptcy."

With the Declaration of Independence, the colonies declared their independence. The independence-minded statesmen who met to decide the wording in the Declaration did not start from scratch. It's ironic that the man whose writings most inspired Thomas Jefferson was an Englishman, political philosopher John Locke (1632–1704). Locke believed that a government should have the popular support of the people and that revolution is justified if the government works against the protection of life, liberty, and property. Under English rule, the colonists were threatened on all three counts.

The Declaration of Independence is divided into the preamble, and second and third sections. The preamble contains the words "all men are created equal." The second section lists the twenty-eight grievances against King George III, and the third section is the resolution for independence proposed by delegate Richard Henry Lee (1732–1794), which begins, "That these United Colonies are, and of Right ought to be Free and Independent States."

Richard Henry Lee

THE DECLARATION OF INDEPENDENCE

When in the Course of human events, it becomes necessary for one people to dissolve the political bands which have connected them with another, and to assume among the powers of the earth, the separate and equal station to which the Laws of Nature and of Nature's God entitle them, a decent respect to the opinions of mankind requires that they should declare the causes which impel them to the separation.—We hold these truths to be self-evident, that all men are created equal, that they are endowed by their Creator with certain unalienable Rights, that among these are Life, Liberty and the pursuit of Happiness.—That to secure these rights, Governments are instituted among Men, deriving their just powers from the consent of the governed.—That whenever any Form of Government becomes destructive of these ends, it is the Right of the People to alter or to abolish it, and to institute new Government, laying its foundation on such principles and organizing its powers in such form, as to them shall seem most likely to effect their Safety and Happiness. Prudence, indeed, will dictate that Governments long established should not be changed for light and transient causes; and accordingly all experience hath shewn, that mankind are more disposed to suffer, while evils are sufferable, than to right themselves by abolishing the forms to which they are accustomed. But when a long train of abuses and usurpations, pursuing invariably the same Object evinces a design to reduce them under absolute Despotism, it is their right, it is their duty, to throw off such Government, and to provide new Guards for their future security. —Such has been the patient sufferance of these Colonies; and such is now the necessity which constrains them to alter their former Systems of Government. The history of the present King of Great Britain is a history of repeated injuries and usurpations, all having in direct object the establishment of an absolute Tyranny over these States. To prove this, let Facts be submitted to a candid world.—He has refused his Assent to Laws, the most wholesome and necessary for the public good.—He has forbidden his Governors to pass Laws of immediate and pressing importance, unless suspended in their operation till his Assent should be obtained; and when so suspended, he has utterly neglected to attend to them.—He has refused to pass other Laws for the accommodation of large districts of people, unless those people would relinquish the right of Representation in the Legislature, a right inestimable to them and formidable to tyrants only.—He has called together legislative bodies at places unusual, uncomfortable, and distant from the depository of their public Records, for the sole purpose of fatiguing them into compliance with his measures.—He has dissolved Representative Houses repeatedly, for opposing with manly firmness his invasions on the rights of the people.—He has refused for a long time, after such dissolutions, to cause others to be elected; whereby the Legislative powers, incapable of Annihilation, have returned to the People at large for their exercise; the State remaining in the meantime exposed to all the dangers of invasion from without, and convulsions within.—He has endeavoured to prevent the population of these States; for that purpose obstructing the Laws for Naturalization of Foreigners; refusing to pass others to encourage their migrations hither, and raising the conditions of new Appropriations of Lands.—He has obstructed the Administration of Justice, by refusing his Assent to Laws for establishing Judiciary powers.—He has made Judges dependent on his Will alone, for the tenure of their offices, and the amount and payment of their salaries.—He has erected a multitude of New Offices, and sent hither swarms of Officers to harass our people, and eat out their substance. He has kept among us, in times of peace, Standing Armies without the Consent of our legislatures.—He has affected to render the Military independent of and superior to the Civil power.—He has combined with others to subject us to a jurisdiction foreign to our constitution, and unacknowledged by our laws; giving his Assent to their Acts of pretended Legislation:—For quartering large bodies of armed troops among us:—For protecting them, by a mock Trial, from punishment for any Murders which they should commit on the Inhabitants of these States:—For cutting off our Trade with all parts of the world:—For imposing Taxes on us without our Consent:—For depriving us in many cases, of the benefits of Trial by Jury:—For transporting us beyond Seas to be tried for pretended offences:—For abolishing the free System of English Laws in a neighbouring Province, establishing therein an Arbitrary government, and enlarging its Boundaries so as to render it at once an example and fit instrument for introducing the same absolute rule into these Colonies:—For taking away our Charters, abolishing our most valuable Laws and altering fundamentally the Forms of our Governments:—For suspending our own Legislatures, and declaring themselves invested with power to legislate for us in all cases whatsoever.—He has abdicated Government here, by declaring us out of his Protection and waging War against us.—He has plundered our seas, ravaged our Coasts, burnt our towns, and destroyed the lives of our people.—He is at this time transporting large Armies of foreign Mercenaries to compleat the works of death, desolation and tyranny, already begun with circumstances of Cruelty & perfidy scarcely paralleled in the most barbarous ages, and totally unworthy the Head of a civilized nation.—He has constrained our fellow Citizens taken Captive on the high Seas to bear Arms against their Country, to become the executioners of their friends and Brethren, or to fall themselves by their Hands.—He has excited domestic insurrections amongst us, and has endeavoured to bring on the inhabitants of our frontiers, the merciless Indian Savages, whose known rule of warfare, is an undistinguished destruction of all ages, sexes and conditions. In every stage of these Oppressions We have Petitioned for Redress in the most humble terms: Our repeated Petitions have been answered only by repeated injury. A Prince, whose character is thus marked by every act which may define a Tyrant, is unfit to be the ruler of a free people. Nor have We been wanting in attentions to our British brethren. We have warned them from time to time of attempts by their legislature to extend an unwarrantable jurisdiction over us. We have reminded them of the circumstances of our emigration and settlement here. We have appealed to their native justice and magnanimity, and we have conjured them by the ties of our common kindred to disavow these usurpations, which would inevitably interrupt our connections and correspondence. They too have been deaf to the voice of justice and of consanguinity. We must, therefore, acquiesce in the necessity, which denounces our Separation, and hold them, as we hold the rest of mankind, Enemies in War, in Peace Friends.—

WE, THEREFORE, the Representatives of the UNITED STATES OF AMERICA, in General Congress, Assembled, appealing to the Supreme Judge of the world for the rectitude of our intentions, do, in the Name, and by Authority of the good People of these Colonies, solemnly publish and declare, That these United Colonies are, and of Right ought to be FREE AND INDEPENDENT STATES; that they are Absolved from all Allegiance to the British Crown, and that all political connection between them and the State of Great Britain, is and ought to be totally dissolved; and that as Free and Independent States, they have full Power to levy War, conclude Peace, contract Alliances, establish Commerce, and to do all other Acts and Things which Independent States may of right do.—And for the support of this Declaration, with a firm reliance on the protection of divine Providence; we mutually pledge to each other our Lives, our Fortunes and our sacred Honor.

A DECLARATION OF INDEPENDENCE IS BORN

~*1776*~

January 9	Fires of independence are fueled by the publication of Thomas Paine's *Common Sense*.
April 12	North Carolina delegates support independence. (In May 1775, Mecklenburg County, North Carolina, first declares its independence.)
June 7	Virginia's Richard Henry Lee submits resolution for independence. Five men are appointed to draft the document: Thomas Jefferson, John Adams, Benjamin Franklin, Roger Sherman, and Robert R. Livingston.
June 7–July 1	The committee of five revises the text.
July 2	Lee's resolution for independence is adopted by Congress; Congress reworks the Declaration.
July 4	Twelve colonies vote for independence; New York abstains. John Hancock and Charles Thomson sign the Declaration. Congress orders the Declaration printed, and the final text is copied on parchment for signing.
July 6	The Declaration appears in the Philadelphia *Evening Post*.
July 8	The Declaration is read publicly in Philadelphia by Colonel John Nixon; the Liberty Bell rings.

July 9	New York finally votes its approval. George Washington reads the Declaration to his troops.
August 2	Most of the fifty-six delegates formally sign the parchment Declaration.

On August 2, 1776, most of the fifty-five signatures on the Declaration of Independence were added to the parchment copy. New delegates signed as late as 1781. One delegate, Robert R. Livingston, one of the original committee of five who drafted the document, was busy drafting New York State's first constitution and never did get around to adding his signature to the Declaration.

PLEDGE

From the Latin word *plebium*, "to pledge," and, later, the Old French *plege*, comes our word *pledge*. If you promise to do something, you, in effect, make a pledge. You can pledge duty to a country or philosophy, or you can pledge your love to someone, as in William Shakespeare's 3 *Henry VI* (act III, scene 3, lines 250–1): "Yes, I accept her, for she well deserves it, And here to pledge my vow, I give my hand." Ben Jonson (1572–1637), English dramatist and poet, wrote perhaps some of the most repeated lines about a pledge. They are from his poem "To Celia": "Drink to me only with thine eyes, And I will pledge with mine."

In the fourteenth century, a hostage, a person who was held against his will, was called a pledge. It's quite the opposite today in American slang. A college student who willingly joins a fraternity or sorority is a pledge.

One of the most well-known pledges is the Pledge of Allegiance, which is repeated facing the American flag. Did you ever wonder who made the first Pledge of Allegiance? This patriotic oath has no connection with the American Revolution or the Fourth of July. It all began in 1892 when Francis Bellamy, a magazine editor in Rome, New York, wrote these words for school children to recite on Columbus Day: "I

pledge allegiance to my Flag and the Republic for which it stands—one nation, indivisible—with liberty and justice for all."

Over three decades later, "my" was changed to "the" Flag. In 1954, President Dwight D. Eisenhower (1890–1969) made another change when he signed a bill that added "under God" after "indivisible."

The French *liberté*, "liberty," from the Latin word *liber*, "free," gives us our word *liberty*. English philosopher John Stuart Mill (1806–1873) wrote in his famous essay "On Liberty": "The modern spirit of liberty is the love of individual independence." The Declaration of Independence states that "all men are created equal, that they are endowed by their Creator with certain inalienable rights, that among these are life, liberty and the pursuit of happiness."

The Liberty Bell, which hangs in Independence Hall in Philadelphia, is one of the most treasured symbols of American liberty. But the famous bell didn't become known as the Liberty Bell until 1839, when the antislavery movement adopted the bell as a symbol of freedom.

Cast in England in 1752, the bell had been ordered by Philadelphia to celebrate the golden jubilee of Pennsylvania's 1701 Charter of Privileges. While being tested, the bell cracked and was recast twice.

Nobody at the signing of the Declaration of Independence even mentioned the bell, and it was finally rung on July eighth. During the Revolutionary War, it was removed and hidden in nearby Allentown. The Liberty Bell, weakened by deep cracks, has not been struck since the anniversary of George Washington's birthday in 1846.

The inscription on the Liberty Bell says in part: "Proclaim liberty throughout all the land." One statesman who proclaimed liberty eloquently in his powerful speeches was Virginia delegate Patrick Henry (1736–1799). In 1775 he spoke these memorable lines: "Forbid it, Almighty God! I know not what course others may take; but as for me, give me liberty or give me death."

Other Famous Wartime Exclamations

"The die is cast," proclaimed Julius Caesar in 49 B.C. as he led his army across the Rubicon River and into Italy.

"Don't fire until you see the whites of their eyes." It's believed William Prescott made this famous statement during the battle of Bunker Hill in June 1775. He was not the first, however. In 1757, Frederick the Great of Prussia commanded his troops: "No firing till you see the whites of their eyes." This was during the Seven Years' War, fought with France, Austria, and Russia.

"I only regret that I have but one life to lose for my country," said brave Captain Nathan Hale (1755–1776) on September 22, 1776, captured when trying to bring back information from behind British lines. He was probably familiar with this passage from *Cato*, a tragedy by English poet Joseph Addison (1672–1719): "What pity is it/That we can die but once to save our country!"

Scotsman John Paul Jones (1747–1792), an American naval officer who fought during the Revolutionary War, on September 23, 1779, cried out from his sinking ship: "I have not yet begun to fight."

62

"We shall go on to the end, we shall fight in France, we shall fight on the seas and oceans, we shall fight with growing confidence and growing strength in the air, we shall defend our island, whatever the cost may be, we shall fight on the beaches, we shall fight on the landing grounds, we shall fight in the fields and in the streets, we shall fight in the hills; we shall never surrender." These are the valiant words of British statesman Winston Churchill (1874–1965), spoken on June 4, 1940.

"I shall return," promised General Douglas MacArthur (1880–1964) when he left the island of Corregidor in the Philippines for Australia on March 11, 1942.

 Do You Know

It specifies in the Declaration that our Creator endows us with certain inalienable rights, such as life and liberty. What, exactly, is an *inalienable* right?

Alien is used when referring to people who are not citizens of the United States. In science-fiction tales, *aliens* are from other planets. The word *alien* comes from the Old French word *alien* and means "belonging to another person or place." The suffix *-able* means "capable of," so if something is *alienable* it is "capable of belonging to someone else." Yet when *alienable* is preceded by the prefix *in*, or "not," the reverse is true: an inalienable right cannot be taken away or transferred.

FREEDOM

Freedom grew out of two Old English words: *freo*, "free," and the suffix *-dom*, "state of being." Freedom is exactly that: the quality or state of being free from slavery or from the power of another. In medieval times there were no abstract freedoms, only tangible ones that could be given and taken away as the feudal lords decided.

It's estimated some 10,000 African-Americans went to battle during the American Revolutionary War, either in the Continental Army or the local militias. Many of them were enslaved men who joined the army in order to gain their freedom and took names in keeping with this goal. Jeffrey Liberty and Jube Freedom are two names from the regimental rolls in Virginia.

In his annual message to the Congress on December 1, 1862, President Abraham Lincoln addressed the issue of freedom and slavery: "In giving freedom to the slave, we assure freedom to the free—honorable alike in what we give and what we preserve."

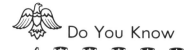

One of the most prominent symbols of American freedom is the Statue of Liberty. Sculpted by Frederic-Auguste Bartholdi (1834–1904), who used his own mother as a model for the head, the statue was a gift from the people of France to the United States to commemorate the alliance between the two countries. At 152 feet high and 225 tons, the copper statue was shipped from France, disassembled, in 200 enormous wooden crates. After being placed on Bedloe's Island (now Liberty Island), the statue was dedicated on October 28, 1886. American poet Emma Lazarus's (1849–1887) renowned lines from her sonnet "The New Colossus"—"Give me your tired, your poor, Your huddled masses yearning to breathe free . . ."—were inscribed on the granite pedestal base in 1903 as a tribute to the thousands of immigrants who sailed past Lady Liberty on their way to nearby Ellis Island.

JUSTICE AND EQUALITY

The Latin words *justitia*, "equality or uprightness" and *justus*, "fair," evolved into the Old French word *justise*, "just," and into English as *justice*.

When you act in a fair manner, you are displaying justice. The Austrian ruler Emperor Ferdinand I (1503–1564) penned this famous thought, usually quoted only in part: "Let justice be done, though the world perish." English poet Alexander Pope's (1688–1744) book of essays *The Dunciad* contains another familiar reference to justice. This one was adopted by many sculptors and painters, and representations are often displayed in and around courts of justice. "Poetic Justice, with her lifted scale; Where, in nice balance, truth with gold she weighs. . . ."

Speakers and writers often mention justice and equality in the same breath. The word *equality* developed from the Latin words *aequalis* and *aequs*, "level and just," which then became *equalite*, "just," in Old French and *equality* in English. Scottish dramatist and creator of the play *Peter Pan*, Sir James Barrie (1860–1937), expressed this thought in another play, *The Admirable Crichton*: "His Lordship may compel us to be equal

upstairs, but there will never be equality in the servants' hall."
In his book *The Subjection of Women*, philosopher John
Stuart Mill addressed another area in which he saw a need
for justice. This work, strongly influenced by his wife, Harriet,
was considered a radical and controversial work for 1869.
"The legal subordination of one sex to the other," wrote Mill,
"is wrong in itself . . . and ought to be replaced by a principle
of perfect equality, admitting no power or privilege on the
one side, nor disability on the other."

 Do You Know

One of the twenty-eight grievances listed in the Declaration of
Independence claims that King George III "obstructed the administration of justice, by refusing his assent to laws for establishing judiciary powers."

Thomas Jefferson also tried to right some wrongs concerning
justice and equality when he wrote the draft for this document.

The preamble states quite clearly that "all men are created
equal." Another of the grievances Jefferson originally listed denounced King George III for supporting the African slave trade.
However, this grievance was eventually dropped from the draft.
Delegates feared that if it remained, both Georgia and South
Carolina, which still permitted the importation of African slaves,
would vote against the Declaration.

Wave the FLAG of RED, WHITE,
and BLUE.
The STARS AND STRIPES
is the national BANNER.

WAVE THE FLAG

No Fourth of July celebration is complete without the waving or flying of the national flag. *Wave* drifted down in English from Old English *wafian*, "to wave or flutter with the hands," related to Old English *woefre*, "restless." A curling movement of water in the sea is called a wave, as is the soft undulating curl in someone's hair. Shel Sand watched the crashing waves, then waved to Julia Beech as waves of wind fluttered through the soft waves of her golden hair.

One theory is that the root of the word *flag* fluttered down from the Middle English word *flagge*, meaning "reed or rush." If you've ever been in a marshy area, you might have seen blue or yellow irises with very narrow grasslike leaves. These flowers are called blue or yellow flag.

Editors call attention to, or flag, errors. A deer's tail is a flag; trainmen signal trains by flagging them; composers add flags on musical notes; masons chisel rocks into thin flagstones. When people lose enthusiasm, they are said to flag. Winston Churchill rallied England's spirits as the country faced a possible German invasion in 1940: "We shall not flag or fail." In this passage from *Romeo and Juliet* (act V, scene 3, lines 94–6), when Romeo laments dead Juliet, William Shakespeare uses *flag* in a symbolic way: "Thou art not conquered;/Beauty's ensign yet/Is crimson in thy lips and in thy cheeks,/And death's pale flag is not advanced there."

The history of the design of the American flag is a rich and complex one. When the English settlers came to America, they brought with them a red flag with a small white upper square (called a canton) set with a cross of St. George, used from the time of Queen Elizabeth I (1533–1603). Later, the X-shaped cross of St. Andrew was added to the English flag.

On January 2, 1776, in Cambridge, Massachusetts, George Washington took command of the newly formed Continental Army. There, angry American patriots burned a copy of King George III's speech, in which he demanded the colonials lay down their arms, and unfurled a flag. This flag, called the "Grand Union Flag," still strongly resembled the flag of Great Britain with its crosses, but there was a dramatic addition: thirteen red and white horizontal stripes. These revolutionary stripes symbolized the union of the thirteen colonies.

How did the flag evolve from the Grand Union flag to the one with thirteen stripes of red and white and a circle of thirteen white stars? You may have heard the story of how a Philadelphia seamstress named Betsy Ross (1752–1836) designed and sewed the first Stars and Stripes.

As the story goes, General Washington visited Mrs. Ross in her tailor shop and discussed plans for a new flag. Yet despite this familiar legend, there's not one shred of evidence to suggest that General Washington (who kept detailed diaries) either met with Mrs. Ross or that she had a hand in designing the new flag. Mrs. Ross did sew flags during the

Revolution, and it seems the sole basis for the story is Betsy Ross herself. On her deathbed at the age of eighty-four, Mrs. Ross told her eleven-year-old grandson that she was Washington's flag seamstress. Thirty years later, her grandson wrote the story up as fact.

The truth is, no one knows for certain who designed the Stars and Stripes. We don't even know when it was first flown. We do know the earliest mention of an American Stars and Stripes was in a congressional resolution dated June 14, 1777, which approved the new flag. June 14 is, of course, the day we celebrate Flag Day. However, the new Stars and Stripes never fluttered over any Revolutionary War battles, since Congress didn't provide General Washington's army with flags until 1783.

 Do You Know

The flag is sometimes called Old Glory. No one knows for sure where the name originated. Suggestions that it may have come from Betsy Ross have been dismissed by historians. One theory is that William Driver, a sea captain from Salem, Massachusetts, first used the phrase when referring to the national flag, but the context is lost.

Next to Betsy Ross, the woman best remembered from the Revolutionary War period is Molly Pitcher. The famous legend that surrounds this woman involves a well near Freehold, New Jersey, the site of the Battle of Monmouth.

According to the story, Molly, born Molly Ludwig, was married to John Hays, a gunner who fought at Monmouth. In the process of drawing water at the well to take to her husband and his comrades, she supposedly saw him fall in battle and valiantly took his place.

According to Revolutionary War historians, the name Molly Pitcher might have come from the fact that people who carried water in military camps were referred to as "pitchers." Although we cannot be certain of the accuracy of the legend surrounding Molly, there's no doubt she existed. It's documented that Molly Ludwig was with the Continental Army at Monmouth and received a pension after the war.

RED, WHITE, AND BLUE

From the Old English *read* comes our word *red*, pronounced to rhyme with "bread." The *a* from *read* was dropped around the twelfth century, but the pronunciation remained. In the New Testament (Matthew 16:2), we are told: "When it is evening, ye say, It will be fair weather: for the sky is red." R. Inwards in his *Weather Lore* gave the scripture's forecast a nautical slant: "Sky red in the morning is a sailor's sure warning; Sky red at night is the sailor's delight."

With its great range of tones, red is often preceded by descriptive words such as blood, fire, rose, cherry, flame, and brick. In centuries past, if you had blood-red cheeks and lips, you were considered healthy. Poet Alexander Pope gives this advice in his poem "Epistle to Lord Cobham": "Betty, give this cheek a little red." The red color on the American flag signifies valor, sacrifice, and blood.

White developed from the Old English word *hwit*, "white, or free of color." A popular phrase is "as white as snow." Its origin is the Old Testament Book of Daniel (7:9): "The Ancient of days did sit, whose garment was white as snow." The flag's white color signifies virtue and unity.

White also conveys purity and innocence. White lies are considered harmless. Metal that is heated until very hot will turn white, so white can also symbolize intense feeling. Jill told a little white lie about her whitewater experience. She turned white as a sheet, and her partner was white with anger, when they capsized in a rapid on the Red River.

Blue made its way into English from the Old English word *blaw* and, later, the French word *bleu*, "blue," or that part of the color spectrum between green and violet. The spelling *blue* was introduced after 1700 due to French influence. In late eighteenth-century Europe, the color blue was associated specifically with American liberty and freedom.

The phrase "to talk a blue streak" means to talk rapidly. In the midnineteenth century, horse-drawn mail coaches moved so quickly that they were said to leave a blue streak behind them. When a month has two full moons, the second one is called a "blue moon." This event, which doesn't happen often, inspired our phrase "once in a blue moon."

 Do You Know

Several other countries have flags that incorporate red, white, and blue in their design, the Netherlands, Czechoslovakia, and France, to name three. Can you identify any others?

STARS AND STRIPES

The word *star* tumbled into English from *steorra*, which evolved from the Greek word *aster*, all meaning "a natural luminous body visible in the sky, especially at night." From *aster* evolved our word *astrology*, "the study of stars," and the Latin *stella*, from which comes *constellation*, "a group of stars." From the moment people first looked up and saw the glittering stars in the heavens, the star became a symbol of hope and aspiration. Don't we, in fact, call someone a "star" when they have reached their highest goals?

Throughout history, stars with at least six rays have decorated family coats of arms in a system called heraldry. A star with five broad triangular points appeared on emblems of Christian chivalry. These five-pointed stars represented the pointed revolving disk at the end of a horseman's spur, called a spur *rowel*. (The word *roulette*, "a spinning wheel of fortune," comes from *rowel*.)

In describing the meaning of the stars on the American flag, George Washington said: "We take the stars from heaven." But some flag historians, called vexilologists, maintain that the stars were not plucked from the heavens but from General Washington's own coat of arms, which featured three five-pointed stars. Others believe five-pointed stars were chosen because seamstress Betsy Ross discovered they were faster to cut out than the six-pointed ones.

The stars' companions, the *stripes*, do not appear in any written texts before the seventeenth century, although the word is thought to be much older. Word historians believe *stripe* grew out of the Old English word *strica*, "streak." A fabric with a streaked pattern is said to be striped.

To George Washington, the white stripes on the American Stars and Stripes "shall go down to posterity representing liberty." The fact that General Washington's family crest had a stripe motif has led some experts to conclude that his heraldry also influenced the stripes on the flag. The marquis de Lafayette, who fought bravely at Washington's side, may have been the first one to call the flag the Stars and Stripes. His son, Georges Washington Motier de Lafayette, was named after the general he served.

 Do You Know

Our national anthem, "The Star-Spangled Banner," was written some thirty-eight years after the American war for independence. *Spangle* comes from the Old English word *spang*, a "shiny ornament." The song was written by a lawyer named Francis Scott Key (1779–1843) during the War of 1812. He was inspired to write the words after witnessing the battle of Fort McHenry, in Maryland's Chesapeake Bay, from a British warship, where he was sent under a short truce to bring back a captured prisoner. Ironically, Key set his famous lines to a familiar British tune, "To Anacreon in Heaven." Although people began singing the song at once, it wasn't until 1931 that the composition officially became America's national anthem, closely beating out "America the Beautiful."

THE STAR-SPANGLED BANNER

Oh, say can you see by the dawn's early light,
What so proudly we hailed at the twilight's last gleaming?
Whose broad stripes and bright stars, thro' the perilous fight,
O'er the ramparts we watched were so gallantly streaming?
And the rockets' red glare, the bombs bursting in air,
Gave proof thro' the night that our flag was still there.
Oh, say does that star-spangled banner yet wave
O'er the land of the free and the home of the brave?

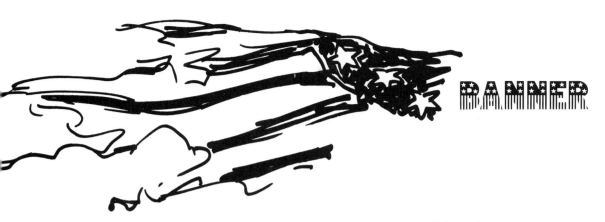

Banner had its beginnings in the Late Latin word *bandum*, or a "standard." *Bandum* grew into both Old French and Old English as *banere*. For centuries, cloth banners have been held aloft as a rallying point for men during battle. "Terrible as an army with banners," announces the Old Testament Song of Solomon (6:4).

During the hard-fought battle for American independence, both the army and navy flew a rich array of flags that represented banners of regiments, individual leaders, states, and, in a few cases, the nation. Among the many motifs incorporated on these flags were a rattlesnake, an eagle, pine and palmetto trees, Indian corn, bleeding military officers, a silver crescent moon, and patriotic slogans.

English poet Lord Byron (1788–1824) took an active role in fighting for independence for both Italy and Greece. Stricken with a fever, Lord Byron died in Greece a century before Greece became independent of Turkey. In his long narrative poem *Childe Harold's Pilgrimage*, Byron's words ring true for America's battle for freedom: "Yet, Freedom! yet thy banner, torn, but flying, Streams like the thunder-storm against the wind."

Lead the BAND, YANKEE
DOODLE DANDY!
UNCLE SAM heads the
FIFE and DRUM corps.

Band marched into English from the late fifteenth-century French word *bande*, "troop," and the Spanish word *banda*, "sash." A company of Spanish soldiers was originally called a *banda* because the men wore colorful ribbon sashes.

Any organized group united in a common purpose is referred to as a band, including those that play musical instruments. *Band* is also used in informal phrases. "When the band begins to play" is a way of saying that things are serious. "To beat the band" means, literally, "to drown out the noise of a band," which means, in effect, you have come out on top, or as the winner.

American marching bands are usually led by a strutting male drum major, from the French word *major*, short for sergeant-major. A female drum major is called the drum majorette. Baton twirlers that often march with bands are called majorettes. In its April 20, 1941, issue, the *San Francisco Examiner* noted a new trend: "During the past few years the drum major . . . has given way to the so-called majorette."

The sport of baton-twirling has its origins in ceremonial dances performed in areas like the Samoan Islands and Thailand. There, dancers flipped and twirled everything from spears to knives as part of the festivities.

Early in the twentieth century, male drum majors started to twirl heavy batons. By the 1930s, female drum majorettes were twirling the lighter, slimmer version in use today.

Although there were no drum majors or twirling majorettes during the American Revolution, bands were very much a part of the military. At the British surrender at Yorktown, General Washington's band had the last word when they struck up the tune "Yankee Doodle." As part of the ceremonial proceedings at Yorktown, the defeated British army put on their best face, marching in brand new uniforms, as they played an old British marching tune that seemed to fit the bill, "The World Turned Upside Down."

YANKEE DOODLE DANDY

The word *Yankee* has many colorful stories associated with its beginnings. According to the *Oxford Dictionary of English Etymology*, the word *Yankee* first appeared around 1683, from the Dutch *Yanke*, "John," a term used by the Dutch or English to ridicule people from New England. Another possibility is that *Yankee* grew out of the word the Indians spoke for "English," *Yengees*. Whatever the word history, we know that British soldiers who wanted to insult New Englanders during the American Revolution called them Yankees.

Doodle can be traced to the German word *dudeltopf*, "a night cap," or, in less formal usage, a "silly fellow," or "simpleton." In English dramatist Samuel Foote's (1720–1777) play *Mayor of Garret*, we read: "Why, doodle, jackanapes harkee, who am I?" How *doodle* got lumped with *Yankee* is another mystery. A ridiculed character in a satire by English novelist Henry Fielding (1707–1754) was named Doodle, so it's thought the British simply added Yankee to Doodle when poking fun at a silly fellow from New England. Today when someone draws in an aimless fashion they are said to doodle.

Dandy's origins are unknown, but the word may be short

for the seventeenth-century English term *Jack-a-Dandy*, someone who dresses elegantly, sometimes excessively. Anyone who wore exaggerated clothing in early nineteenth-century London was called a dandy. Irish romantic poet Thomas Moore (1779–1852) described his dandy this way: "They've made him a Dandy,/A thing, you know, whiskered, greatcoated, and laced,/Like an hour-glass, exceedingly small in the waist." In our country, *dandy* also means fine or splendid.

 Do You Know

The tune for "Yankee Doodle" is usually attributed to a British fifer. The question of who wrote the words—an English surgeon or British soldiers in America—may never be resolved. Musicologists have no doubt, however, that the lyrics were intended to comically depict the differences between the dapper English soldiers and the shabby colonial army.

According to the words of "Yankee Doodle," Yankee Doodle sticks a feather in his cap and calls it "macaroni." Why is the feather called "macaroni"? The "macaroni" in question is not pasta but an eighteenth-century English organization called the Macaroni Club. Its members wanted to import the elegance and sophistication of Europe to England, including fashion and Italian noodles. The fact that poor ragamuffin Yankee Doodle thought the feather an elegant touch made him even more ridiculous in the eyes of the British.

Yankee Doodle came to town
Riding on a pony;
Stuck a feather in his cap
And called it Macaroni.

UNCLE SAM

We all recognize Uncle Sam, the thin man in the flowing beard, flamboyantly dressed like an American flag in red-striped pants and a stars-and-stripe top hat. The word ancestry of *uncle* goes back to the Old French word *oncle*, "uncle," and the Latin *avunculus*, "mother's brother," which gives us our word *avuncular*, "like an uncle." Our phrase "to cry [or say] uncle" is "to admit defeat," as exemplified in American writer Budd Schulberg's (1914–) novel *What Makes Sammy Run?*: "Kit was the one who did him some good. 'Okay,' I said, 'I'll cry uncle.' "

Sam is a shortened form, or nickname, for Samuel. *Samuel* comes from the Hebrew *Shemuel*, the name of the Hebrew judge who anointed both king Saul and David.

Up until three decades ago, any claims that Uncle Sam was

based on a real-life person were totally unfounded. This all changed in 1961, when a historian uncovered a newspaper article from 1830 that contained a firsthand account of how the legend began.

In 1812, Samuel Wilson of Troy, New York, was supplying the United States army with pork and beef. Before the crates of army meat left the plant, they were stamped "U.S.," meaning they were headed for the "United States" army. This was long before it became popular to refer to the United States as the U.S.

A postmaster who was touring the plant with a meat inspector overheard one of the workers respond to a question about what the initials U.S. stood for. The worker replied, possibly jokingly, that the initials stood for Uncle Sam, or Sam Wilson, the meat provider.

Whether the worker was serious or not, the phrase caught on, and soon U.S. soldiers began referring to any military issue they received as coming from their Uncle Sam. A 1960s congressional act declared that "Uncle Sam" Wilson was, indeed, the real-life ancestor of America's national symbol.

When the first picture of Uncle Sam appeared in the newspapers in the early nineteenth century, he had no beard and sported a funereal black top hat and coat. It has not been established whether the first Uncle Sam looked anything like Sam Wilson or not. Over the years, Uncle Sam acquired distinctive physical characteristics and his patriotic dress. During the Civil War, cartoon artist Thomas Nast (1840–1902) depicted Uncle Sam as a tall, gaunt, bearded figure, using

President Abraham Lincoln as a model.

Besides Uncle Sam and the Stars and Stripes, another recognized symbol of the United States is the eagle. In the ancient world, a gold eagle was associated with the most powerful of the Roman gods, Jupiter.

The identification of the bald eagle with the United States can be traced back to 1734. Then, an elderly Creek Indian chief presented a handful of bald eagle feathers to King George II in England as a sign of everlasting peace. He told the king that the feathers were taken from a swift bird that represented power in the land.

It seemed natural, therefore, that the bald eagle, which stood for both independence and strength, was adopted as this country's national symbol to adorn the Great Seal. The bald eagle was chosen over the objections of Benjamin Franklin, who preferred the turkey instead. Franklin disliked the bird's predatory nature and called the eagle a bird of bad character. For him the homely turkey was less offensive.

The design of the Great Seal of the United States began in 1776 and took twelve years to finish. In its talons, the eagle clutches the arrows of war and an olive branch of peace.

FIFE AND DRUM

Trill the fife and beat the drum
Independence Day is come!

The word *fife* first appeared in the fifteenth century, either from the German word *pfeife*, "pipe," or the French *fifre*, "fife." In sixteenth-century England, *drum* had developed with its modern spelling, coming from the Old German word for "drum," *trumme*.

Small, six-holed instruments with a sound so shrill it is said to "shake green apples off trees," fifes were played at ancient Greek and Roman celebrations. Drums, even older than fifes, were introduced into orchestras by the Egyptians around 2000 B.C. "To beat the drum" is a figurative term meaning "to advertise."

By the fifteenth century, fifers and drummers accompanied outdoor dances. About this same time, the military, especially foot regiments, engaged fifers to play lively tunes, which were said to put soldiers in the right spirit for fighting. Musical duties of the fifer also included setting the pace during marches. The song "Yankee Doodle" may have been composed by the fife-major of the Grenadier Guards, an elite English fighting corps. Together, fifers and drummers performed an important duty in calling out various signals during battle, among them "The Assembly," "The March," "The Reveille," "The Retreat," "To Arms," and "The Parley," from the French word *parler*, "to talk."

Following the British lead, regiments in the Continental Army sounded their wooden fifes and drums. At the British surrender at Yorktown on October 19, 1781, a lone red-coated English drummer beat out "The Parley," a signal that conveyed to the other side "we want to talk terms." Although the British officially surrendered, the Treaty of Paris that ended the war was not signed until September 3, 1783.

But the interest in performing military music of the revolutionary period lives on, especially in New England, where today there are some 2,500 active fife and drum corps. Many of these musicians can be seen trilling and beating during local Fourth of July parades, dressed either in fancy hats and suits or more homespun peasant attire. Both are considered historically accurate.

Let's plan
FIREWORKS and a BARBECUE.
At the PICNIC, enjoy a
HAMBURGER and HOT DOG,
POTATO SALAD and
BAKED BEANS,
CHERRY PIE
and WATERMELON.

FIREWORKS

For many, the most dazzling and heart-pounding part of any Fourth of July celebration is the fireworks display that begins at dusk. The two words that make up the word *fireworks* come to us from two Old English words, *fyr*, "fire," and *werc*, "work." Fireworks are also called *pyrotechnics*, from two Greek words, *pyr*, "fire," and *techne*, "art."

The "art of fire" originated in China in the tenth century, when a cook mixed together three ordinary kitchen ingredients of the day—sulfur, charcoal, and saltpeter (a preservative salt)—and produced explosive sparks. Although historians do not know what the chef was trying to concoct, what he actually produced was history's first gunpowder.

The Chinese soon discovered that if they packed this mixture into a hollowed-out bamboo tube, they could fire rockets into the air. The Chinese used these explosives to celebrate weddings, moon eclipses, the new year, and to ward off evil spirits. Three centuries later, a German monk named Berthold Schwarz used gunpowder to fire the first gun.

As early as 1532, Charles V (1500–1558), ruler of the Holy Roman Empire, hired fireworks technicians, called fireworkers, to stage elaborate displays of pyrotechnics to celebrate his military victories. At the beginning of the seventeenth century, fireworkers created sophisticated devices known as

set pieces, which when lit formed silhouettes of complete scenes and courtly figures. In 1664, Louis XIV's (1638–1715) fireworkers illuminated an entire battle between three sea monsters at Versailles palace. One French fireworker shot rockets containing mice and rats into the air, after which the animals descended under small parachutes.

One of the most extravagant fireworks pageants in this country was held on July 4, 1876, in New York, when every building was outlined against a background of shooting rockets. Another occurred on May 15, 1983, when a niagara of colorful lights tumbled down from the Brooklyn Bridge during the bridge's hundredth-birthday shindig.

 Do You Know

DIFFERENT TYPES OF
FIREWORKS

BATTLE IN THE CLOUDS

Shells that explode in a series of loud bangs, giving the impression of a battle; popular at Italian festivals

FIRECRACKERS

Small, usually cylindrically shaped explosives strung together that explode on the ground in sharp bangs; often heard at Chinese New Year celebrations

SHELL

Canisters fired out of a mortar that explode in flowery star bursts; common at large civil displays

GIRANDOLE (from the Italian *girandola*, "to turn")

A cluster of rockets that spin a disk up and off a center pole and into the air like a flying saucer

CHERRY BOMB

Powerful, round red firecracker that is outlawed in the United States

ROCKET

Cone-shaped cylinder attached to a long stick that soars high into the air when lit

ROMAN CANDLE

Tubes stuck into the ground that when lit send stars into the air; so called because the Romans supposedly featured them at carnivals

SET PIECE

Wooden contraptions set with lances that when illuminated form the outline of a person or scene in colored fire; the largest set piece ever constructed was at London's Crystal Palace in 1898 and depicted the destruction of the Spanish fleet by the English, covering 60,000 square feet

CATHERINE WHEEL

Set pieces that revolve in different kaleidoscopic color combinations; the wheel was named for a fourth-century Egyptian woman who refusing to renounce her Christianity was tortured on a spiked wheel by order of Roman emperor Maxentius.

SPARKLER

A narrow steel wire that when lit sends out a shower of fine gold sparks

Fireworks are not toys and accidents related to their use can be serious.

97

BARBECUE

Another Fourth of July tradition, the *barbecue*, comes from the Spanish word *barbacoa*, "a stick framework on posts." The idea that the popular spelling *barbeque* evolved from the French phrase *barbe à queue* makes no sense when you consider the French words translate as "beard to tail."

In the seventeenth century, if you struck a match to your barbecue, you might have burned up your bed! At this time, the crude raised platform on which people slept was referred to as a barbecue. People at this time also smoked and dried raw meat on similar wood structures also called barbecues.

In the following century, any animal that was broiled or roasted whole was referred to as a barbecue. Later, the term was applied to the social gathering rather than the food. In Jamaica, a barbecue has nothing at all to do with grilling meat or an outdoor party. There a barbecue is the name of the house where coffee beans are laid out to dry.

PICNIC

Picnic, from the French word *pique-nique*, first appeared in the 1740s in Europe and around 1800 in England. According to its original meaning, if you invited your friends for a picnic at your house, your guests were expected to pitch in by bringing their share of the food. These were fashionable entertainments that usually took place inside.

Later, in the midnineteenth century, the meaning of *picnic* changed slightly. Guests still contributed part of the menu, but the picnics were held in a country setting. Eventually, contributing food to the picnic was not expected and this meaning was dropped from the word. Now picnic refers to a gathering of friends eating outside. Another term for eating out of doors is *alfresco*, Italian for "in the open air."

If you told a friend that writing your book report was a real picnic, it means you had an easy time doing it. And vice versa: getting all the food on the small picnic table at the barbecue was no picnic.

HAMBURGER AND HOT DOG

What could be more American than grilling hamburgers and hot dogs on the barbecue! Yet from a word-history point of view, there's absolutely nothing American about either of these favorite Fourth of July foods.

The word *Hamburger* refers specifically to someone who lives in the German seaport town of Hamburg. A popular food in fourteenth-century Germany was shredded beef mixed with spices and served either cooked or raw. In the town of Hamburg, this dish became known as "Hamburg steak." German immigrants brought the dish to America in the 1880s, and by the time it was served up at the 1904 World's Fair in St. Louis, the beef patty—its name abbreviated to *hamburg*—was sandwiched in a bun. By the 1930s, a chain of White Castle hamburger restaurants had spread across America.

As inseparable as Uncle Sam and the Fourth of July are hamburgers and their barbecue partners, hot dogs. *Hot dog* got its start from two Old English words, *hat*, "hot," and *docga*, "dog." A nineteenth-century German butcher named George Lahner is credited for developing a sausage in Frankfurt, the *frankfurter*, and one in Vienna, the *wiener*. German immigrants took Lahner's sausages to America, along with the hamburger steak.

In the 1880s, concession stands at Brooklyn's seaside resort Coney Island sold these German sausages as "Coney Island red hots." A few years later, at the Polo Grounds, home of baseball's New York Giants, the vendors in the bleachers yelled out: "Get your red-hot dachshund sausages!" After all, franks are curved like the long, skinny dachshund dog. The "dachshund dog" was shortened to "hot dog" when a newspaper cartoonist forgot how to spell *dachshund* as he labeled a cartoon of a mustard-smeared dachshund in a bun. So he simply captioned it "hot dog." Americans eat an astounding 16 billion hot dogs every year.

In American slang, anyone who performs in a skillful but show-off manner is considered a "hot dogger." This is especially true of surfers and skiers. "Hot dog" and "hot diggety dog" are both slang expressions of delight or approval.

 Do You Know

Frankfurter, after Frankfurt, Germany, and *wiener*, for Vienna, Austria, and the earlier *boycott*, for Captain Boycott, are all eponymous words. The word *eponymous* is a combination of two Greek words, *epi*, "after," and *onyma*, "name." Words that are "named after" someone or something are said to be eponymous. Here are some other eponymous words:

WORD	ORIGIN	NAMED AFTER
sandwich	late eighteenth-century England	John Montagu, earl of Sandwich
Melba toast	late nineteenth-century England	opera singer Helen Porter Mitchell, known as Nellie Melba because she came from Melbourne, Australia
teddy bear	early twentieth-century United States	President Theodore Roosevelt
Frisbee	midtwentieth-century United States	William Russell Frisbie, late nineteenth-century Bridgeport, Connecticut, baker His pies sat on flat circular tins embossed with the name Frisbie
mackintosh	1820s Scotland	Charles Mackintosh, designer
leotard	nineteenth-century France	trapeze artist Jules Leotard

POTATO SALAD AND BAKED BEANS

Next to rice, more potatoes are eaten in the world than any other food. The origin of the word *potato* is the Spanish word *batata*, "potato," which was adopted from Taino, a Caribbean language now extinct.

Although we know the word history of *potato*, we don't know for sure who grew the first potato—or where. Potatoes were first brought to America by Spaniards landing in the West Indies around 1500. These potatoes were what we call sweet potatoes. Irish people who fled Ireland for New England in 1719 brought with them white potatoes, later called Irish potatoes, and paid their rents in pecks of potatoes.

The Latin word *sal*, "salt," evolved into the Old Provençal words *sal*, "salt," *salar*, "to salt," and then *salada*, a dish of salted vegetables, especially lettuce or cress. If someone talks about their "salad days," they are probably not discussing lettuce. The phrase refers to a time of youth and green inexperience. It may have been used first by Cleopatra in William Shakespeare's *Antony and Cleopatra* (act I, scene 5, lines 73–4): "My salad days, When I was green in judgement: cold in blood."

The dish that most often shares a plate with potato salad is, of course, tangy baked beans. *Baked beans* came into English from two Old English words, *bacan*, "bake," and *bean*, "bean," the edible vegetable pod. The most famous baked beans in the United States are those called Boston baked beans, and because of this association, the city of Boston has been nicknamed Beantown.

Most food historians agree that this traditional dish of navy beans, salt pork, and molasses was introduced to the American colonists by Indian tribes in the Northeast. The Indians added maple syrup and bear fat to the beans and then slow-cooked them inside a deer hide, which was set in an underground pit "fireplace." The colonists substituted molasses and salt pork in their version.

Like *potato*, the word *bean* is part of many colorful expressions. It's believed the Romans fed beans to their horses. From this we get the phrase "full of beans," which describes someone raring to go, like a horse that's just eaten. "Not worth a hill of beans" is another way of saying "small potatoes," or something of little value. "Hill of beans" goes back to the thirteenth century, when Robert of Gloucester said "not worth a bean" in his *English Chronicles*. "Spill the beans" or "telling what you know" is a slang phrase usually reserved for tough action movies. And if you "don't have a bean," you're broke. That spills all the beans on the subject of beans in slang—and in tomato sauce.

Do You Know

Although potato salad is a staple at American picnics, the stuff that binds it together is Old World. In the 1700s, a French duke sampled a delicate sauce made of egg yolk and olive oil in Mahon, Minorca, an island off Spain. The French called it *mahonnaise* after Mahon. The sauce arrived in America as *mayonnaise* in the early 1800s. Considered far too difficult for the average cook to prepare in the preblender days, mayonnaise became a staple only when delicatessen-owner Richard Hellman bottled his Hellman's mayonnaise in 1912.

When Thomas Jefferson was ambassador to France, he ate thickly cut, fried potatoes that became known as French fries. A lover of good cuisine, he brought these delicious-tasting French fries back to America with him and served them to his guests at his home, Monticello.

CHERRY PIE

Cherry developed from the Latin word *cerasus*, "cherry tree." According to Roman writers, a wealthy Roman named Lucullus, famous for his love of food, brought these fruit trees to Rome from nearby Cerasus.

If you ordered a piece of pie before English Queen Elizabeth I's time, you would have received a main course: a pastry stuffed with meat or fish. The original fruit dessert pie can be traced back to Elizabeth herself. One evening, the queen specifically asked that the pie crusts be filled with pitted, preserved cherries instead of the usual meat filling.

The first fruit to be tucked between pastry in the United States was the apple, thus our phrase "as American as apple pie." But cherry pies have always had a more patriotic flavor to them, probably because of the association of cherry trees with the first president, George Washington.

Most readers are no doubt familiar with the story of how six-year-old George Washington chopped down the cherry tree and then said he could not tell a lie. The story first appeared in clergyman and biographer Parson Weems's (1759–1825) book *Life and Memorable Actions of George Washington*.

Parson Weems never claimed to have witnessed the incident himself, and historians consider it suspicious that he waited until Washington was dead before he put the story in the fifth edition of his book. Weems heard the tale from an "excellent lady." According to the excellent lady, young George did not cut down the prized cherry tree but only hacked at the trunk with his hatchet. Further, when confronted, George was carrying his new hatchet. Caught red-handed, he confessed, "I can't tell a lie, Pa."

 Do You Know

George Washington isn't the only well-known figure to get involved with a tale concerning fruit. Two others are William Tell, the legendary national hero of fourteenth-century Switzerland, and English mathematician Sir Isaac Newton (1642–1727). William Tell supposedly lived during a time when Austria governed Switzerland. Tell became a hero when he refused to salute the Austrian imperial governor. For punishment, he was forced to try to shoot an apple off the head of his own son with a crossbow. Tell's aim was accurate, but he was still thrown into prison. The tale ends with peasants rescuing Tell, who went on to lead Switzerland to freedom from Austrian rule.

Isaac Newton is probably best known for his discovery of the law of gravity, and he is often pictured next to a falling apple. Any connection between the fall of an apple and his scientific conclusions can be traced back to a story first told by French poet and dramatist Voltaire (1694–1778). Voltaire claimed to have heard it directly from Sir Isaac Newton's niece.

WATERMELON

Watermelon is made up of the Old English word *waeter*, "water," and Latin *melopepo*, "melon," which developed in French and Spanish as *melon*. One of the earliest descriptions of this juicy fruit goes back to 1666, in J. Davies's book *History of the Carivbby Islands*: "There grows in these countries another kind of melons . . . call'd Water-Melons, because they are full of a sugar'd water, intermingled with their meat."

"To cut the melon" is slang for deciding a question. Another slang melon involves "melon cutting," which refers to dividing or sharing profits in stock transactions or betting. This item appeared in the October 7, 1909 issue of the *New York Evening Post*: "A purse of $25,000 will be distributed among employees. About 8,000 men will participate in the cutting of the melon."

A cake popular in America nearly a century ago was called watermelon cake. The cake batter was pink to resemble the flesh of the watermelon, and raisins were added as "seeds." The recipe as it appeared in cookbooks from the turn of the century called for red sugar and special baking pans and rings.

Here's an updated version easy enough for everyone to make. Note: If you know someone who bakes specialty cakes, ask to borrow an oval-shaped pan to recreate the watermelon shape.

Fourth of July Watermelon Cake

Use your favorite boxed white cake mix, or a recipe from scratch, to make two eight-inch cake layers. Add one cup of raisins or currants to the batter after the dried ingredients have been thoroughly mixed. Tint the white cake batter a deep pink by adding a few drops of red food coloring.

While the layers are baking, prepare enough white icing for a two-layer cake, or use premixed icing. Mix a few drops of green food coloring into white icing to tint it a pale green. If you like, reserve one-third of the white icing and drizzle lines down the green icing to imitate the stripes on a watermelon skin.

Cut one slice from the cake before serving so that everyone will get the full "watermelon" effect.

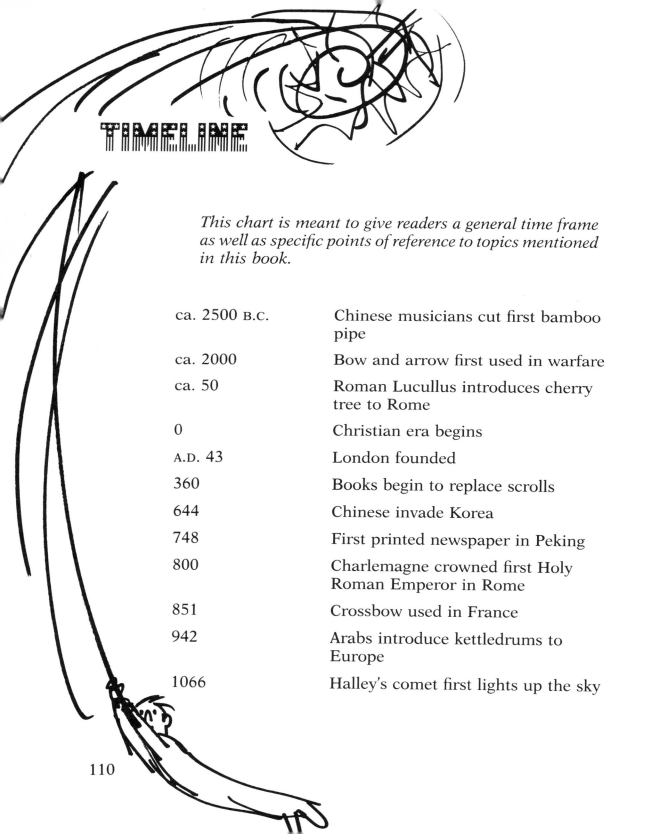

TIMELINE

This chart is meant to give readers a general time frame as well as specific points of reference to topics mentioned in this book.

ca. 2500 B.C.	Chinese musicians cut first bamboo pipe
ca. 2000	Bow and arrow first used in warfare
ca. 50	Roman Lucullus introduces cherry tree to Rome
0	Christian era begins
A.D. 43	London founded
360	Books begin to replace scrolls
644	Chinese invade Korea
748	First printed newspaper in Peking
800	Charlemagne crowned first Holy Roman Emperor in Rome
851	Crossbow used in France
942	Arabs introduce kettledrums to Europe
1066	Halley's comet first lights up the sky

ca. 1200	Chinese set off first fireworks
1218	Oldest national flag in the world adopted by Denmark
1313	Berthold Schwarz uses gunpowder in a firearm
1519	Charles V crowned as head of the Holy Roman Empire
1664	Louis XIV spends 1 million dollars on fireworks
1721	Swedish settlers bring rifles to U.S.
1749	Bonnie Prince Charlie (Charles Edward Stuart) leads Scotland in revolt against England but is defeated at the Battle of Culloden

★ ★ ★ REVOLUTIONARY CALENDAR ★ ★ ★

October 1767	Boston agrees not to import British goods
June 1768	Corrupt customs officials seize John Hancock's ship *Liberty*; anti-British feeling peaks in Boston
October 1768	British soldiers land in Boston
May 1769	Virginia votes to close ports to British imports

March 5, 1770	Boston Massacre—British soldier accidentally fires on angry mob; 3 patriots die, 2 mortally wounded
May 1773	British Tea Act gives tea monopoly to East India Co.
December 16, 1773	Disguised as Indians, Boston citizens throw tea cargo into Boston Harbor
June 1774	Britain closes Boston Harbor
October 14, 1774	Congress adopts Declaration of Rights and Grievances
April 19, 1775	Battles of Lexington and Concord
June 15, 1775	George Washington appointed commander-in-chief of Continental Army
June 17, 1775	British win at Bunker Hill
July 6, 1775	Congress adopts a Declaration of the Causes and Necessity of Taking Up Arms
July 8, 1775	Olive Branch petition sent to King George III, offering reconciliation
July 26, 1775	Postal system established
September 1, 1775	July 8 petition rejected by King George III
January 1, 1776	Continental flag (with thirteen stripes) raised at Washington's headquarters at Cambridge

July 2, 1776	Congress adopts Virginia delegate Richard Henry Lee's resolution for independence
July 4, 1776	Jefferson's draft of the Declaration of Independence is adopted by Congress
October 19, 1783	British Lord Cornwallis surrenders to General George Washington at Yorktown

★ ★ ★ ★ ★

1783	Congress issues first American Stars and Stripes flags
1787	U.S. Constitution signed
1789–1799	French Revolution
1812	U.S. declares war on England
1814	Napoleon I banished to Elba
1822	Brazil becomes independent of Portugal
1823	Mexico becomes a republic
1829	Turkey acknowledges Greek independence
1833	Slavery abolished in England
1861	U.S. Civil War begins
1862	Emancipation Proclamation frees slaves in the Confederacy

1876	Korea becomes independent
1900	Hot dogs sold at U.S. baseball games
1904	The ice-cream cone first appears at St. Louis World's Fair
1917	Russian revolution against Czar Nicholas II
1924	Greece becomes a republic
1929	Michigan is first state to pass legislation prohibiting fireworks
1935	First major baton-twirling contest in Chicago, Illinois
1948	U.S. Selective Service Act sets up peacetime draft
1950	North Korea invades South Korea
1963	Kenya becomes an independent republic; United Arab Republic-Syria-Iraq union
1976	North and South Vietnam are reunited; Seychelles Islands declare independence from England
1983	Firework artist spends $800,000 in Portuguese display
1990	East and West Germany unite
1991	U.S. and its allies declare war on Iraq after invasion of Kuwait

BIBLIOGRAPHY

ETYMOLOGY

C. T. Onions, ed. *The Oxford Dictionary of English Etymology*. Oxford: Clarendon Press, 1966.
> A standard for anyone interested in the history of the English language, compiled by one of the staff members of the original OED.

The Oxford English Dictionary. Second edition. Oxford: Clarendon Press, 1989.
> This authoritative twenty-volume dictionary of word etymologies not only provides the historical record of how words have developed and changed meaning but offers literary quotations that are as illuminating as they are fascinating.

Shipley, Joseph T. *Dictionary of Word Origins*. New York: Philosophical Library, 1945.
> Word histories plus some anecdotal material in short, very digestible entries.

HISTORY AND INFORMATION

Bakeless, Katherine and John. *Signers of the Declaration*. Boston: Houghton Mifflin, 1969.
> Describes the fifty-six signers of the Declaration of Independence.

Boorstin, Daniel J. *The Landmark History of the American People*. New York: Random House, 1968.
> A highly readable account that explores the human side of American history, written by one of this country's greatest historians.

Cunliffe, Marcus. *George Washington, Man and Monument*. Boston: Little, Brown, 1958.

A fascinating and illuminating account that scrapes through myth to unveil the "moral" Washington.

Hays, Wilma Pitchford. *Freedom*. New York: Coward-McCann, 1958.

Reproductions of twenty-six significant documents pertaining to American history and their background. The book can be placed in an opaque projector for screen magnification in the classroom.

Panati, Charles. *Extraordinary Origins of Everyday Things*. New York: Harper & Row, 1987.

An entertaining and enlightening survey that points out the origins of over five hundred everyday items. The stories behind them are unfailingly fascinating.

Plimpton, George. *Fireworks*. New York: Doubleday, 1984.

Written by the unofficial fireworks commissioner of New York City, this book sparkles with Plimpton's enthusiasm and wide knowledge of all manner of pyrotechnics that have lit up the night sky for centuries.

Stember, Sol. *The Bicentennial Guide to the American Revolution*, volumes I–III. New York: Saturday Review Press/E. P. Dutton, 1974.

Without a doubt, the most superlative guide to some 600 American Revolution sites, a must-read guide for anyone interested in exploring battlefields, forts, and monuments.

SUGGESTIONS FOR ADDITIONAL READING

Asimov, Isaac. *The Kite that Won the Revolution*. Boston: Houghton Mifflin, 1963.

Bliven, Bruce, Jr. *The American Revolution, 1760–1783*. New York: Random House, 1958.

Cohen, Hennig, and Tristram Potter Coffin, eds. *The Folklore of American Holidays*. Detroit: Gale Research, 1987.

Dalgliesh, Alice. *The Fourth of July Story*. New York: Charles Scribner's Sons, 1956.

Fritz, Jean. *Will You Sign Here, John Hancock*. New York: Coward McCann & Geoghegan, 1976.

Mastai, Boleslaw, and Marie-Louise D'Otrange. *The Stars and the Stripes*. New York: Alfred A. Knopf, 1973.

Morris, Richard B. *The Making of a Nation*. New York: Time, 1963.

Strick, Lisa W. *The Black Presence in the Era of the American Revolution, 1770–1800*. Washington, D.C.: Smithsonian Institution, 1973.

Tuleja, Tad. *Curious Customs*. New York: Harmony Books, 1987.

INDEX

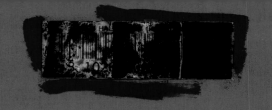